In memory of

Jeff Herr

Given by

Mount de Chantal
Class of 1973

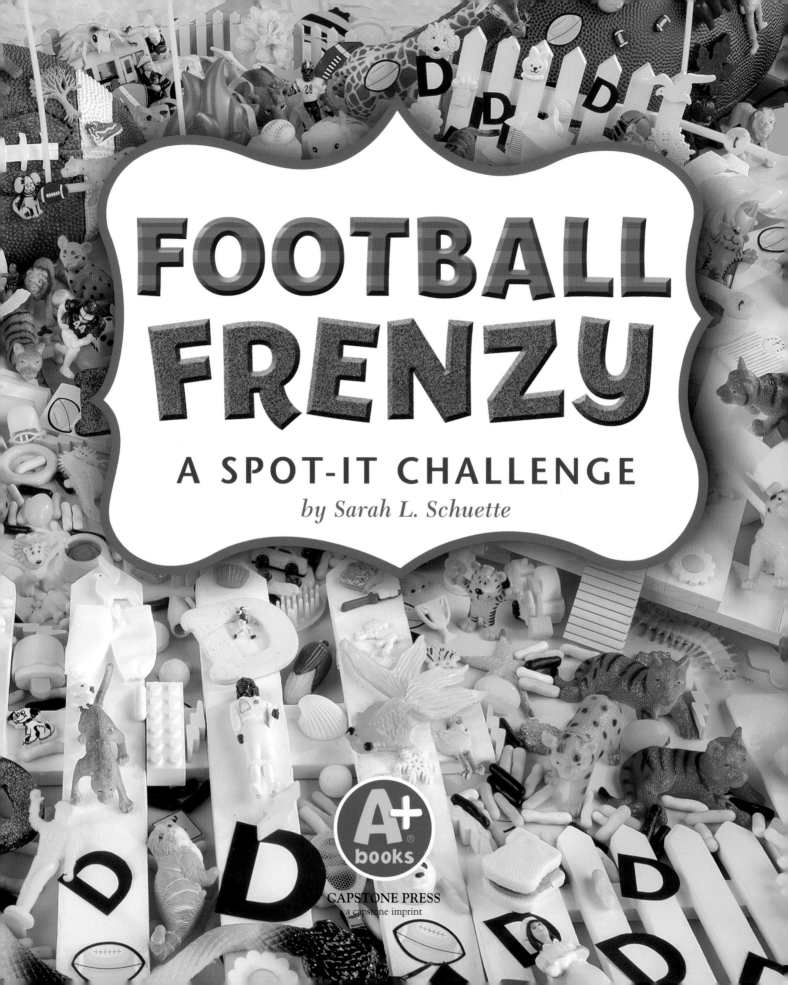

FOOTBALL FRENZY

A SPOT-IT CHALLENGE

by Sarah L. Schuette

A+ books

CAPSTONE PRESS
a capstone imprint

A+ Books are published by Capstone Press,
1710 Roe Crest Drive, North Mankato, Minnesota 56003
www.capstonepub.com

Library of Congress Cataloging-in-Publication Data
CIP information is on file with the Library of Congress.
ISBN: 978-1-62065-062-2 (library binding)
ISBN: 978-1-4765-1350-8 (eBook PDF)

Editorial Credits
Jeni Wittrock, editor; Juliette Peters, designer; Wanda Winch, media researcher;
Laura Manthe, production specialist

Photo Credits
All photos by Capstone Studio: Karon Dubke

The author dedicates this book to Ian Thomas Todd of Brownton, Minnesota.

Note to Parents, Teachers, and Librarians
Spot It is an interactive series that supports literacy development and reading enjoyment.
Readers utilize visual discrimination skills to find objects among fun-to-peruse photographs
with busy backgrounds. Readers also build vocabulary through thematic groupings,
develop visual memory ability through repeated readings, and improve strategic and
associative thinking skills by experimenting with different visual search methods.

Printed in the United States of America in North Mankato, Minnesota.
092012   006933CGS13

Table of Contents

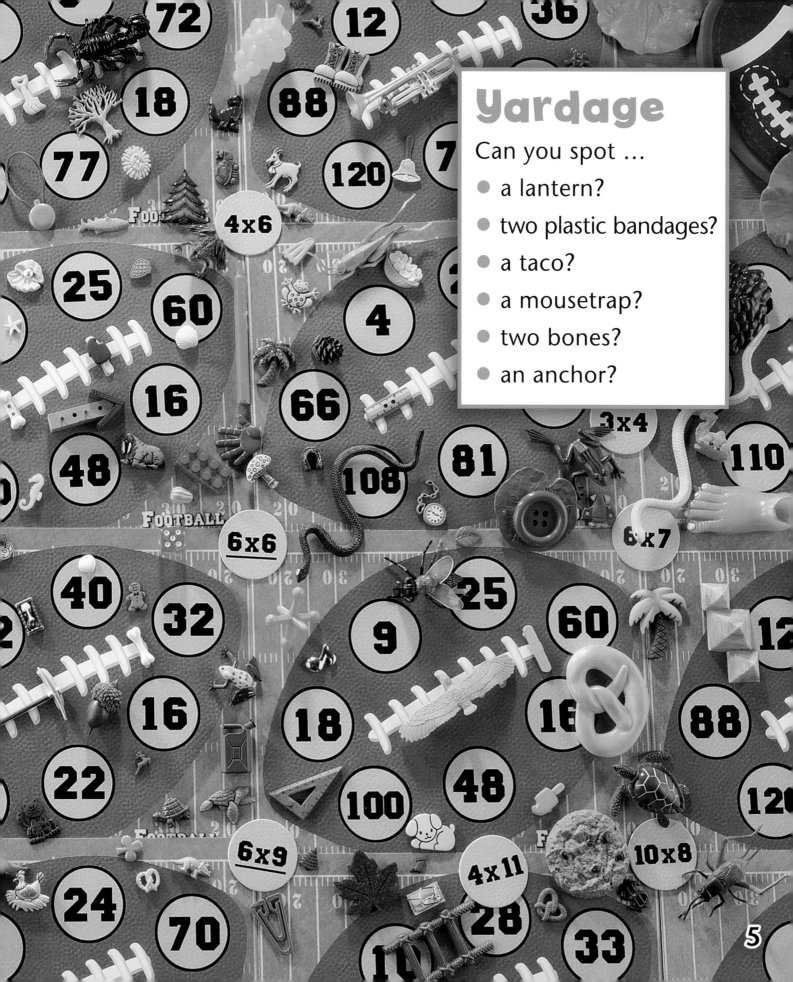

Yardage

Can you spot ...
- a lantern?
- two plastic bandages?
- a taco?
- a mousetrap?
- two bones?
- an anchor?

Touchdown

Can you spot ...

- a cowboy hat?
- a cactus?
- a fish bone?
- the letter "H"?
- a flamingo?
- a pencil?

Uniforms

Can you spot …

- a walrus?
- a unicycle?
- a snowman?
- an eyeball?
- a kangaroo?
- two milk bottles?

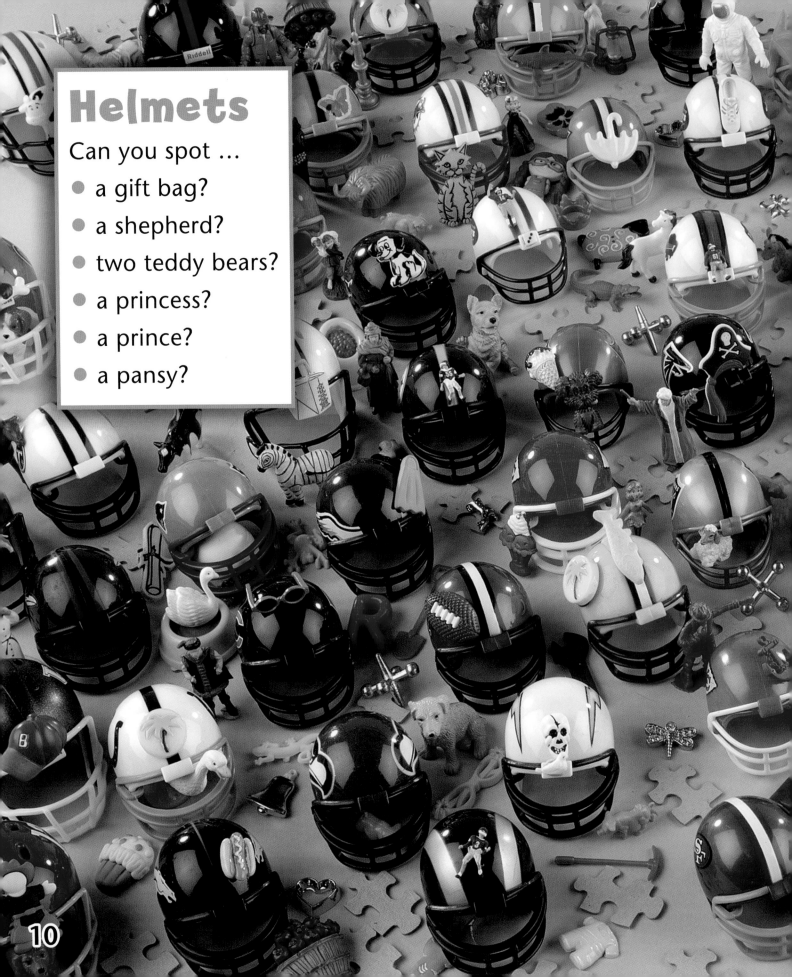

Helmets

Can you spot …
- a gift bag?
- a shepherd?
- two teddy bears?
- a princess?
- a prince?
- a pansy?

Huddle Up

Can you spot …

- two mittens?
- an Army tank?
- two dinosaurs?
- a wheelbarrow?
- a tomato?
- a butterfly?

Defense

Can you spot …

- a trumpet?
- a trophy?
- a chef's hat?
- a ring?
- two zebras?
- a wind surfer?

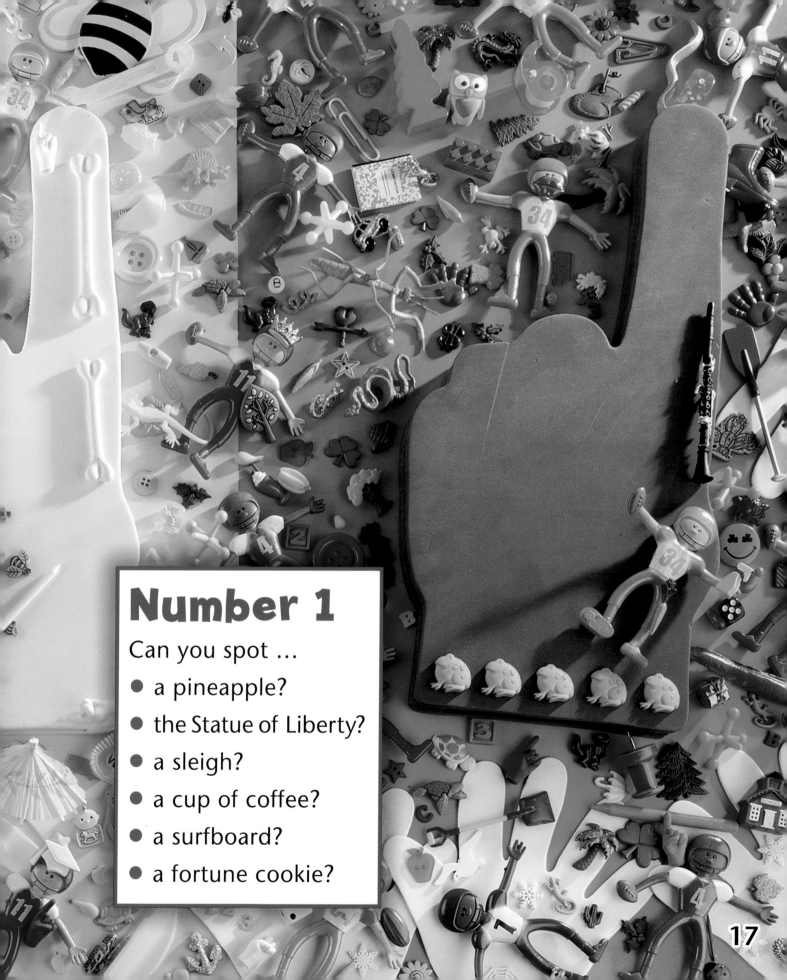

Number 1

Can you spot ...

- a pineapple?
- the Statue of Liberty?
- a sleigh?
- a cup of coffee?
- a surfboard?
- a fortune cookie?

Vintage

Can you spot …

- a toaster?
- a pinecone?
- a violin?
- two hamburgers?
- a buffalo?
- a skunk?

Game On

Can you spot ...

- a treasure map?
- a mailbox?
- two crowns?
- a ghost?
- a hanger?
- a bathtub?

Tailgate

Can you spot ...

- a peapod?
- a campfire?
- a cupid?
- a horseshoe?
- two hair dryers?
- a roll of toilet paper?

22

Halftime

Can you spot ...

- a cell phone?
- an astronaut?
- a slice of bread?
- a patio chair?
- a croissant?
- a crayon?

Mascots

Can you spot ...
- a raspberry?
- a pumpkin?
- a key?
- a steak?
- two guitars?
- a paintbrush?

Spot Even More!

Yardage

Try to spot an ear of corn, a baseball bat, a money sign, two popsicles, and two rulers.

Touchdown

This time find a pair of lips, a stingray, a guinea pig, two rabbits, and an umbrella.

Uniforms

See if you can find a covered wagon, two snowflakes, a sandwich, and a battleship.

Helmets

Try to find an orange, an ice-cream sundae, a dog food dish, a swan, and an arrow.

Huddle Up

Now spot a head of lettuce, a genie lamp, an ice-cream sandwich, and a weather vane.

Defense

Time to find an ear, a jackhammer, a maple leaf, a waffle, and a panda.

Number 1

Now look for two pairs of sunglasses, a wizard's hat, a roll of tape, and a graduation hat.

Vintage

Check for a swing set, two camels, an oil barrel, a cowboy, two gladiators, and a grill.

Game On

Try to find a baby bottle, two toucans, a witch's hat, a helicopter, and a pair of binoculars.

Tailgate

Take another look to find a golf tee, a wrench, an eggplant, two pairs of scissors, and three canoes.

Halftime

See if you can spot a pirate ship, two watermelons, two roses, a hand mirror, and a farm wagon.

Mascots

See if you can spot a hermit crab, an acorn, a pair of gloves, a sandcastle, and a mushroom.

Extreme Spot-It Challenge

Just can't get enough Spot-It action? Here's an extra football challenge. Try to spot:

- a piece of pizza
- a doughnut
- a chili pepper
- five strawberries
- an igloo
- a pretzel
- a bunch of grapes
- a purse
- a carrot
- a palm tree
- a koala
- a sun
- a hair brush
- two hotdogs
- a tent
- a crab
- two bunches of bananas

Read More

Mahaney, Ian F. *The Math of Football.* Sports Math.
New York: Powerkids Press, 2012.

Schuette, Sarah L. *Sports Zone: A Spot-It Challenge.*
Spot It. North Mankato, Minn.: Capstone, 2013.

Wyatt, James. *Football.* On the Team.
New York: Gareth Stevens Pub., 2012.

Internet Sites

FactHound offers a safe, fun way to find Internet sites
related to this book. All of the sites on FactHound
have been researched by our staff.

Here's all you do:

Visit *www.facthound.com*

Type in this code: 9781620650622

Super-cool stuff! Check out projects, games and lots more at
www.capstonekids.com